ALTERNATOR BOOKS™

THE MOON FILES

THE MOON'S IMPACT ON OUR EARTH

Beth Adelman

Lerner Publications ◆ Minneapolis

This book is dedicated to everyone who stops and looks up at the night sky.

Lerner Publications Company
An imprint of Lerner Publishing Group, Inc.
241 First Avenue North
Minneapolis, MN 55401 USA

For reading levels and more information, look up this title at www.lernerbooks.com.

Main body text set in Aptifer Sans LT Pro.
Typeface provided by Linotype.

Library of Congress Cataloging-in-Publication Data

Names: Adelman, Beth, author.
Title: The moon's impact on our Earth / Beth Adelman.
Description: Minneapolis, MN : Lerner Publications, [2025] | Series: Alternator books. The moon files | Includes bibliographical references and index. | Audience: Ages 8–12 | Audience: Grades 4–6 | Summary: "The moon affects life on Earth in many ways. From the ocean tides to animal migration, discover how the moon causes change on Earth and what would happen if we didn't have the moon"—Provided by publisher.
Identifiers: LCCN 2023048881 (print) | LCCN 2023048882 (ebook) | ISBN 9798765625606 (library binding) | ISBN 9798765629833 (paperback) | ISBN 9798765638002 (epub)
Subjects: LCSH: Moon—Juvenile literature. | Moon—Phases—Juvenile literature. | Earth (Planet)—Juvenile literature.
Classification: LCC QB582 .A338 2025 (print) | LCC QB582 (ebook) | DDC 525—dc23/eng/20231108

LC record available at https://lccn.loc.gov/2023048881
LC ebook record available at https://lccn.loc.gov/2023048882

Manufactured in the United States of America
1 – CG – 7/15/24

TABLE OF CONTENTS

Life on Earth would be much different without the moon.

INTRODUCTION

IS THE MOON IMPORTANT?

The moon is so far away that it takes astronauts about three days to fly there. It doesn't seem like something so far away would affect us much on Earth. Our night sky would be a lot darker without the moon. But would anything else really be different if the moon wasn't there?

The answer is yes! Without the moon, Earth would be a very different place. Our days would be much shorter. Our seasons would not be predictable. Many animals would not know when to have babies. Other animals would not know where to go during migrations. Even humans would not fare well if Earth had no moon.

How does the moon affect life on Earth? Let's find out!

It is 238,900 miles (384,472 km) from Earth to the moon.

Scientists suggest that our moon was born when the planet Theia collided with Earth.

CHAPTER 1

SETTING THE SEASONS

Scientists think our moon formed about 4.5 billion years ago, when a planet about the size of Mars crashed into Earth. Most of that planet was blown to bits in the collision. But parts of it mixed with exploded parts of Earth. Eventually, they clumped together to form the moon.

The moon is a little more than one-fourth the size of Earth. That's a lot bigger than most other moons in our solar system. Other moons are much smaller than the planets they orbit. Bigger, more solid objects have stronger gravity. Our moon's strong gravity has kept our seasons and our days stable.

Scientists think that when the moon formed, a day on Earth was just six hours long. That's because Earth was rotating much faster. The gravity of the moon helped slow it down. So, the moon helped make our 24-hour day.

THE RABBIT IN THE MOON

Some people think the light and dark areas on the moon resemble the face of a smiling man. That's the man in the moon. In parts of Asia, they see a rabbit. The Salish of the northwest coast of the US see a toad. In the Philippines, it's a woman with her hair up. In Malaysia it's a tree. When you look at the moon, what do you see?

Different cultures see different people, shapes, or objects in the moon's dark and light areas.

Wobble and Spin

If you drew a line straight through Earth from the north pole to the south pole, that line is Earth's axis. We know that Earth's axis is tilted. The giant crash that formed the moon is probably what made it tilt.

This tilt is why we have seasons. When the axis tilts toward the sun, it's summer. When it tilts away, it's winter.

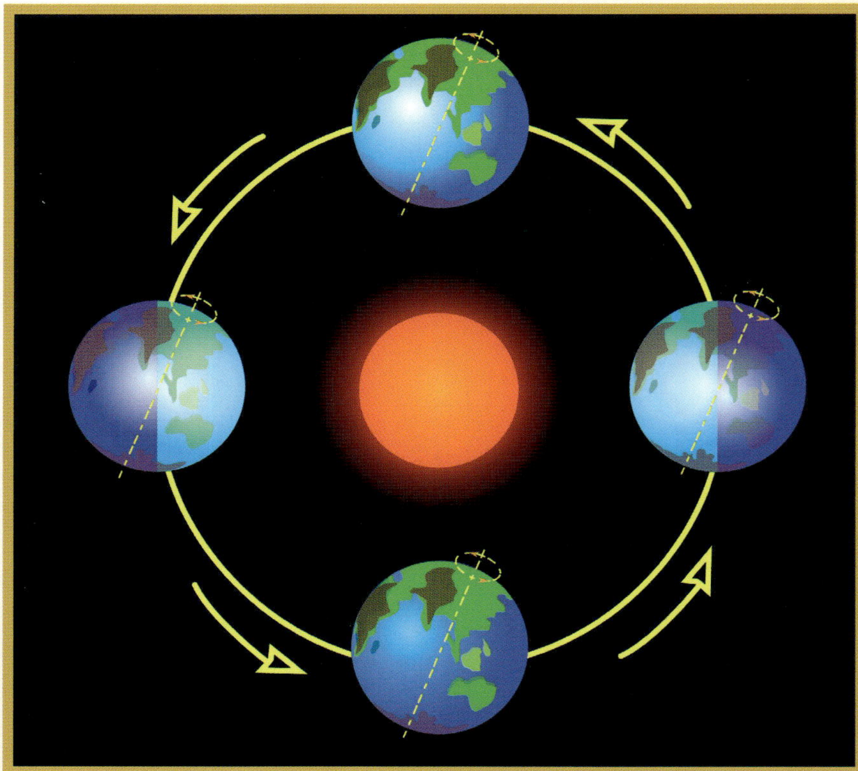

Earth's seasons change as it rotates on its axis.

Other planets, such as Mars, have much smaller moons that ours.

As Earth rotates, it wobbles a little on its axis. That's because Earth is not perfectly round. Imagine spinning a basketball on your finger. The perfectly round ball stays on your fingertip. But if you stuck a big wad of chewing gum on one side of the ball, the weight of the gum would pull the ball over.

The wobble of Earth's axis is very small. Earth does not fall over, though. That's because the gravity of the moon helps keep it stable.

A wobbly Earth would make weather unstable at the North and South Poles.

Calming Our Climate

Without our big moon to stabilize Earth's wobble, the axis could point straight up and down. It could be side to side other times. That means sometimes it would be freezing at the north and south poles and super hot at the equator. And other times it would be freezing at the equator and super hot at the poles.

Extreme climate changes would happen often throughout the year without the moon to keep Earth stable. All the living things on Earth would have to adapt to these extreme changes. Humans and most animals would probably not be able to live in a world like that. Without the moon, Earth might be home to nothing but very simple plants and bacteria.

Cold weather at Earth's equator would cause big problems.

Each ocean coast has two high tides and two low tides every day.

CHAPTER 2

TURNING THE TIDES

As the moon orbits Earth, sometimes it's closer to one side of our planet. Sometimes the moon is closer to the other side of Earth. The moon's gravity is stronger on the side of Earth it is closest to. That stronger gravity pulls Earth's oceans toward the moon, making a bulge.

This bulge creates high tides, where the ocean comes up to its highest point on the shore. Because of the force generated when Earth spins, the water also bulges on the opposite side of Earth at the same time. So, there are high tides on that side of Earth, too. This explains why the tides change twice in a 24-hour day.

As Earth and the moon move, the water in the ocean sloshes back and forth like water in a giant bathtub. When the ocean sloshes up in one place, it goes down in another. Where it goes down is a low tide.

When the tide comes in, it pushes more water toward the beach. This means bigger waves and better surfing!

When Life Began

The sun's gravity also affects the tides. But the sun's influence is about half as strong as the moon's. The difference between high tide and low tide would be much less if we had no moon.

Billions of years ago, the moon was ten times closer to Earth. The tides were one thousand times higher. And because Earth was spinning faster, there were high tides every three hours.

These super tides eroded coastal areas, adding minerals from the rocks and soil to the oceans. Scientists believe those minerals were very important for the evolution of the first life forms.

The sun's impact on tides is about half that of the moon.

Tides affect erosion along the coasts.

The moon cycles through eight phases once a month.

CHAPTER 3
TELLING TIME

In the deep winter, when days are short and cold, ancient people may have wondered, "Will the weather ever get warmer? When will the plants give us food again?" To figure this out, they counted how much time had passed in each season and

then how many days were ahead. They did this by watching the phases of the moon.

When we look at the moon, we see only the part that is lit by the sun. Because Earth and the moon keep moving, the angles between them and the sun keep changing. From Earth, it looks like the moon disappears and then grows from a sliver to a full moon and back. This cycle from no moon to full moon and back to no moon takes about 29.53 days.

The Phases of the Moon

Early people used the phases of the moon to create calendars. These lunar calendars helped them count the months and years. And it made it possible for them to record their history and plan for the future.

The earliest lunar calendar may date all the way back to 32,000 BCE. It's a piece of bone marked with what scientists think is a record of the phases of the moon. It was found in a cave in central Europe. There are also pictures in caves in France that are 15,000 years old showing the phases of the moon.

An early calendar recorded the days of the moon's cycle on bone.

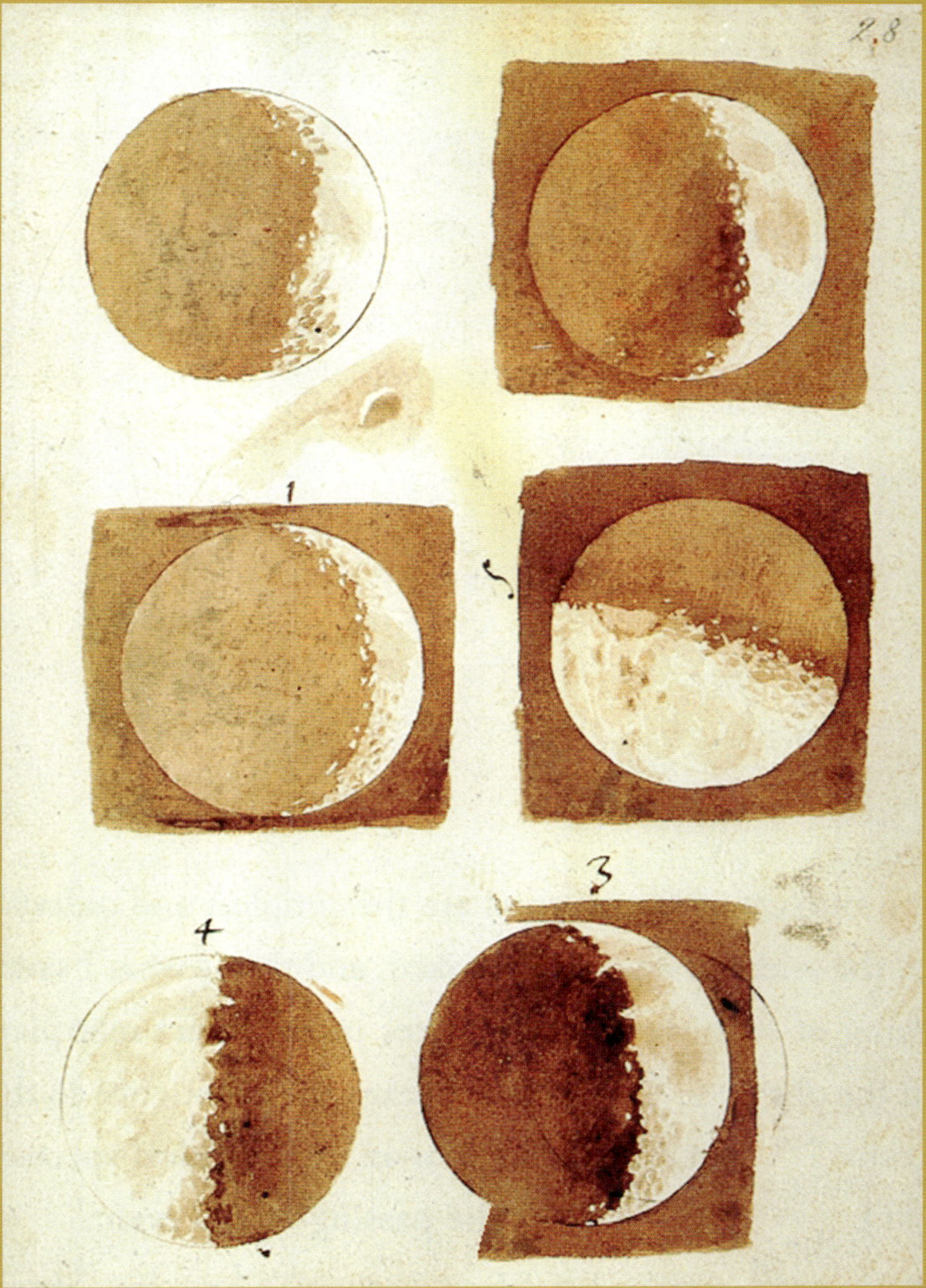

Astronomer Galileo Galilei recorded his observations of the moon phases in the early 1600s.

The First Science

We use a calendar that is based on Earth's orbit around the sun. This is more accurate for keeping track of the seasons. That's because the seasons are caused by Earth's position relative to the sun. Earth completes one orbit around the sun in 365 days, which is

Our modern calendar is based on Earth's orbit around the sun.

the length of a year. But 12 moon cycles take only about 354 days.

Recording the moon's phases helped ancient people begin to understand how to count time. It also taught them how to carefully observe what was going on in their world and note what they saw. They used those notes to make predictions about the future. That is the basis for all scientific research.

Ephedra plants are pollinated when the moon is full.

CHAPTER 4

GUIDING ANIMALS

The phases of the moon affect some birds, fish, mammals, and insects. Scientists are studying how animal behaviors change as the moon changes. They have found that many important animal activities follow the moon.

THE MOON EVEN AFFECTS PLANTS

The green ephedra makes little cones that must be pollinated. Under the full moon, each cone produces a droplet of fluid to stick its pollen to passing insects. These droplets sparkle in the moonlight. The light attracts insects. The plant only produces these droplets when the moon is full. And in all plants, sap flows more strongly as the moon becomes full and slows down as the moon gets smaller.

Scientists know that moon phases affect hormone levels in animals. Hormones influence when animals sleep, get hungry, reproduce, are more active, and do other behaviors. But exactly how the moon affects hormone levels is unknown. Its gravity might be the trigger. It might be changes in the amount of moonlight. Or it might be something else.

A full moon increases sap flow in plants and trees.

Insects in the Moonlight

Dung beetles live in grasslands, where food and water are scarce. They eat dung (poop). When the beetles find dung, they shape it into a ball and roll it away to their underground hideout. That is where they can safely enjoy their feast.

Dung beetles travel to their hideout in a straight line, using moonlight to navigate. They follow the specific pattern of moonlight to find their way.

A dung beetle gathers dinner.

A full moon signals doodlebugs to dig bigger holes.

Doodlebugs dig holes in the ground to trap insects to eat. They make their holes bigger around the full moon. Scientists thought this was because more of the insects they eat are active under the full moon. But even in a completely dark laboratory, doodlebugs dig bigger holes when the moon is full. Scientists haven't figured out how doodlebugs know the moon is full when they can't even see it.

Birds Find Their Way

The moon guides many birds on their long migration from one place to another as the seasons change. Barau's petrel, a seabird, breeds on the island of Réunion in the Indian Ocean. The petrels spend the rest of the year in different places. All the petrels wait until the day is exactly 12.5 hours long before setting off for Réunion. And they all arrive together at the full moon.

In the fall, when European nightjars fly south from Sweden to warmer spots, they start their journey about 10 days after the full moon. Individual birds all start off at about the same time, even if they live far apart.

The stars and moon help birds find their way when migrating.

Nightjars begin their migration at the same time.

A full moon signals that it is time for coral species to spawn.

Under the Sea

Once a year, corals around the world spawn. They have the best chance of making baby corals if they spawn at the same time. They time their spawning by the temperature and saltiness of the oceans and by the full moon.

Oysters are more open during new moons and more closed when the moon is full. They even seem to know the difference between the half moon when the moon is growing larger, and the half moon when the moon is growing smaller. They open more when the moon is growing smaller. Scientists don't know why.

The moon guides all these animals, and many more. Without it, Earth would not be the same planet we know today.

Oysters open and close during parts of the moon's cycles.

GLOSSARY

erosion: the process of being worn away by wind, water, and other natural forces

evolution: the process by which living things change and develop from earlier life forms

gravity: the force that attracts all objects to one another

hormones: chemical substances the body produces that act as messengers, helping to control how cells and organs function

orbit: the curved path of one object in space as it travels around another object in space

phases of the moon: the different shapes of the sunlit portion of the moon, which we see at different times of the month

pollinate: to move pollen from one part of a plant to another, so the plant can reproduce

rotate: to spin around a central axis

sap: the fluid in plants

spawn: to release eggs for reproduction

LEARN MORE

Buxner, Sanlyn, Pamela Gay, and Georgiana Kramer. *The Moon*. New York: DK Children, 2022.

Explore Marvel Moon: Dance of the Moon and Oceans
https://www.lpi.usra.edu/education/explore/marvelMoon/activities/whatIf/dance/

Explore Marvel Moon: The Moon's Influence on Us
https://www.lpi.usra.edu/education/explore/marvelMoon/background/moon-influence/

Hirsch, Rebecca E. *Mysteries of the Moon*. Minneapolis: Lerner Publications, 2021.

Huddleston, Emma. *Explore the Moon*. Minneapolis: Kids Core, an imprint of ABDO Publishing, 2022.

Institute of Physics: How does the Moon affect the Earth?
https://www.iop.org/explore-physics/moon/how-does-moon-affect-earth

NASA Space Place: What Are the Moon's Phases?
https://spaceplace.nasa.gov/moon-phases/en/

Rajczak, Michael. *Reaching the Moon*. New York: Gareth Stevens, 2021.

INDEX

PHOTO ACKNOWLEDGMENTS

Image Credits: Interior; Helen Field/Shutterstock, Interior; TB3XNW/Alamy; Interior; titoOnz/Alamy, p. 4; Evgeniyqw/iStockphoto, p. 5; Sergey Nivens/Shutterstock, p. 6; Sergey Nivens/Shutterstock, p. 7; NASA, p. 8; GraphicsRF.com/Shutterstock, p. 9; Vadim Sadovski/Shutterstock, p. 10; Ziga Plahutar/iStockphoto, p.11; ibraman3012/iStockphoto, p. 12; Benny Marty/Shutterstock, p. 13; EpicStockMedia/Shutterstock, p. 14; jpa1999/iStockphoto, p. 15; Ethan Daniels/Shutterstock, p. 16-17; draganab/iStockphoto, p. 18; Marie-Lan Nguyen/Wikimedia Commons, p. 19; Barbara Herrenkind/Wikimedia Commons, p. 20-21; adventtr/iStockphoto, p. 22; Israel Hervas Bengochea/Shutterstock, p. 23; golubka57/Shutterstock, p.24; Natalie colette kilian/Shutterstock, p. 25, Jonas Vegele/Shutterstock, p. 26–27 ; Phillipe Clement/Shutterstock, p. 26; Kurit afshen/Shutterstock, p. 28; SergeUWPhoto/Shutterstock, p. 29; Pix Box/Shutterstock.

Cover: Mike Pellinni/Shutterstock